PENGUIN BOOKS
THE NANNY KIT

Kimberly Porrazzo drew on her ten years' experience in human resources management when she founded the Southern California Nanny Center to assist parents in hiring their own nannies. Ms. Porrazzo and *The Nanny Kit,* her do-it-yourself guide for hiring and managing a nanny, have been featured on the *Today* show and the *CBS Evening News,* and have appeared in the pages of *Business Week, Working Mother, Smart Money,* and *Parents* magazines. She also hosts a website (www.sandcastleweb.com/nanny) that offers parents suggestions for hiring in-home child care. Porrazzo lectures frequently on "How to Hire Your Own Nanny." She lives in Lake Forest, California, with her husband and two children.

The Nanny Kit

Everything You Need to Hire the Right Nanny

Kimberly Porrazzo

Penguin Books

PENGUIN BOOKS
Published by the Penguin Group
Penguin Putnam Inc., 375 Hudson Street,
New York, New York 10014, U.S.A.
Penguin Books Ltd, 27 Wrights Lane,
London W8 5TZ, England
Penguin Books Australia Ltd, Ringwood,
Victoria, Australia
Penguin Books Canada Ltd, 10 Alcorn Avenue,
Toronto, Ontario, Canada M4V 3B2
Penguin Books (N.Z.) Ltd, 182–190 Wairau Road,
Auckland 10, New Zealand

Penguin Books Ltd, Registered Offices:
Harmondsworth, Middlesex, England

First published in the United States of America by The Southern California Nanny Center 1992
This updated edition published in Penguin Books 1999
1   3   5   7   9   10   8   6   4   2
Copyright © Kimberly Porrazzo, 1992, 1999
All rights reserved

A Note to the Reader

This publication is created to provide accurate and authoritative information in regard to the subject matter covered. It is sold with the understanding that the author and the publisher are not engaged in rendering legal, accounting, or other professional advice. If expert assistance is required, the service of a competent professional person should be sought.

LIBRARY OF CONGRESS CATALOGING IN PUBLICATION DATA
Porrazzo, Kimberly
    The nanny kit: everything you need to hire the right nanny / Kimberly Porrazzo.
        p.   cm.
    Includes bibliographical references and index.
    ISBN 0 14 02.7723 4
    1. Nannies—Selection and appointment—United States—Handbooks, manuals, etc.
    2. Nannies—Employment—United States—Handbooks, manuals, etc.   I. Title.
HQ778.63.P67   1999
649'.1—dc21   98–30841

Printed in the United States of America
Set in Minion and Cafeteria
Designed by Jaye Zimet

This book is dedicated, first, to my two sons, Anthony Vincent and Nicholas Thomas, whose love has inspired me.

Second, to my parents, who have always made me feel as if I was their highest priority.

Third, to my husband, Keith, whose love and patience have allowed me to pursue this project over the years.

Finally, to the victims of society's most brutal crime, child abuse, to whom a portion of the profits of this book are dedicated.

Contents

Introduction

If you're reading this book, you've probably already made the decision that you need help caring for your children. Perhaps you're going back to work and are in need of full-time child care. You might be working from your home office and need someone to look after the children while you're trying to conduct business. Maybe you are an at-home parent who just needs help. In any case, you've decided that you need a nanny. Now what?

If you're like most parents, you've probably already made a few phone calls to nanny placement agencies listed in your local telephone directory. Perhaps, like me, you were dissatisfied with the information many agencies provided. High placements fees, limited services, and minimal guarantees left *this* mom reluctant to turn over the important task of finding a nanny for my children to a so-called professional agency, especially in an unregulated industry where the term "professional" is yet to be defined.

These days, more parents are choosing to hire their own nanny. They know what they want for their children, and they're willing to invest the time and energy required to find it. However, for parents who choose to hire on their own, there are few resources available to guide them through each important step of the process. Finding the right nanny involves more than just seeking someone to become a part of your family. It requires you to recruit, interview, and screen nannies with the same professionalism that you expect in a nanny.

In the business world, a candidate for even the lowest entry-level position is put through an entire battery of tests, including skills tests, drug tests, reference checks, and personality profiles. Yet when hiring a nanny, many parents aren't sure what to ask or how to go about checking the nanny's background. Providing that information is precisely the purpose of *The Nanny Kit.*

The Nanny Kit applies the same personnel selection techniques used every day in the business world and adapts them for use in the home environment. It will assist you in recruiting, screening, interviewing, selecting, and managing your nanny. It includes forms that you can use, including a nanny application, reference-checking guides, and evaluation forms. Using this book, you will be sure that you are doing everything possible to conduct a thorough and professional search. No one is more qualified than you to decide who is the right person to care for your child.

Selecting a nanny wisely and professionally is the best beginning to a long, happy relationship with your child's caregiver. The Nanny Kit provides open dialogues and clear expectations that are keys to keeping your nanny happy and motivated. It includes a checklist of responsibilities, a written work agreement, and a daily log sheet that allow the nanny to report back to you at the end of each day concerning your child's behavior, appetite, naps, and activities.

We've also included helpful tips for situations you may encounter after hiring your nanny, such as performance reviews and secret video surveillance. What if you have to fire her? Follow the steps in The Nanny Kit to protect your home and family.

You have all the tools you'll need. Let's get started!

How to Use This Workbook

You will notice that this workbook has plenty of white space. Use this space for note-taking. For example, as you are reading the section on placing an ad for a nanny, use the blank space to write down the newspapers you will advertise in, their phone numbers, and their rates.

As you read through the chapters on paying taxes and insurance coverage, jot down questions you have for your tax consultant and insurance representative, as they apply to your personal situation.

Remember, the objective of this book is to "arm" you with the information you need to ask the right questions, not only of your nanny, but also of other resources you will need to draw upon to properly hire and employ a nanny for your children.

The forms in this book are meant to be copied for your personal use. Keep the originals clean so that you can use them again in the future.

The Nanny Kit

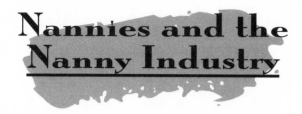

Nannies and the Nanny Industry

The Nanny Industry

As a parent and a consumer, you may be surprised to learn that the nanny industry in the United States is virtually unregulated. In England, nannies must be educated, serve internships, and earn a nursery nurse certificate that qualifies them to work, but here in the United States, *anyone* can be a nanny. There are no educational requirements, no special training programs, no necessary mandatory certification procedures. To apply and be hired for a position as a nanny, it is not even necessary to have any experience in child care.

This is particularly disconcerting when you consider that a manicurist must be trained, serve an internship, be tested, and be licensed in order to legally apply fingernail polish to our fingertips! A manicurist is monitored by the health department. She must renew her license, and her license can be revoked for cause. Yet nothing is required of the people who care for our children in our homes and are responsible for their safety and well-being.

In addition, most states do not regulate nanny placement agencies either. In states where agencies are not licensed, anyone can open a nanny agency and begin to place nannies without state oversight. No laws or regulations govern the selection of your nanny. Most agencies check a nanny's references. Some agencies do background checks on nannies to look for a criminal record or a poor driving record. Others do not.

If you are concerned about hiring a nanny, you may be tempted to bring in the "professionals"—to call an agency. But it may be that no one is more qualified to select a nanny than you are.

Domestic Child Care Titles

There remains a great deal of confusion over titles for domestic child care employees. You may not know what you are getting when you hire a nanny. Will she cook and clean as well? Here are some helpful definitions.

Baby-sitter

A baby-sitter "sits" with children. She looks out for their safety and tends to their needs as requested by the parents. She generally does not have a great deal of child care experience and does not consider this to be her profession. Baby-sitters are usually paid hourly and are hired on a time-to-time basis.

Nanny

A nanny can work full-time or part-time and either live in (with the family) or live out (and commute to work each day). A nanny *nurtures* "her" children, planning activities and outings, reading to them, teaching them, etc. She is responsible for the children and their needs, both physical and emotional. She considers this to be her career. She generally has a good deal of experience, perhaps even training in child development or education, and she can provide several references.

Au Pair

An au pair (pronounced "o-pair") is a young person from abroad—often from Europe—who is invited into a home to care for the children. In exchange, the family offers the au pair a unique cultural experience.

Au pairs usually range in age from 18 to 25 and are hoping to explore our country through an au pair exchange program. Their child care experience is usually limited to having cared for younger siblings or cousins in their own country. Child care is usually a means to an end for them—not a professional interest or a long-term commitment.

In the United States, au pairs may be placed legally only through one of eight authorized au pair agencies. These agencies are monitored by the U.S. Information Agency (USIA).

An au pair cannot work more than the maximum number of hours per week mandated by the USIA. Your commitment to an au pair includes a minimum salary, her own room, health coverage, and payment of tuition for education or a cultural exchange program in the United States. Under this program, au pairs can commit to only one year of service with a family, after which they must return to their home country.

Governess

A governess is a caregiver responsible not only for the safety and well-being of her charges, but also in part for their education, usually as a tutor for children of school age. She plans activities that are not only fun but also educational.

Housekeeper

A housekeeper has the primary responsibility for running a household. She generally handles the cleaning, grocery shopping, cooking, and laundry. She will look after the children, but her ultimate concern is the smooth functioning of the household.

Mother's Helper

A mother's helper is usually brought into a home after a mother has returned from the hospital. The helper assists with the new baby or other young children. She is not left alone with the children, but she does care for the children while the mother is home and requires help. She is a short-term helper and is paid by the hour.

Working with a Nanny Agency

There is nothing a nanny agency does that you cannot do on your own. Agencies have no magic formula for finding nannies, and many follow the same procedures outlined in this book. While nanny agencies do recruit and prescreen nannies, ultimately the parent is still responsible for interviewing, double-checking references, and reviewing background profiles on any nanny an agency refers to them.

In cases where parents do decide to turn over the responsibility of selecting a nanny to an agency, the parents should select that agency as carefully as they would select a nanny. To get the best from an agency, it is imperative that parents retain control throughout the search. Often, new parents who are unfamiliar with the process of hiring in-home help rely solely on an agency for its "expertise," when in fact the individual running the agency may not have the same high standards as the parents. Following this section are questions to ask and a checklist of information; this material can help you find an agency that meets your needs.

Typically, a nanny agency will send several candidates to your home for you to interview. Sometimes the interviews take place in the agency's office. Before these candidates are presented to you, they should have already cleared some preliminary screening and should meet your basic requirements. The purpose of the interview should be only to determine how you feel about the nanny as well as to determine her interest in your position. Some agencies will not do a background check on a nanny unless you indicate an interest in hiring her. Once you elect to make an offer, pending the results of the background check, a work agreement should be drawn up by the agency detailing the parameters of the position. Then the nanny begins work.

Nanny Agency Placement Fees

The fee you owe a nanny agency is often a percentage of the nanny's monthly salary. If you settle on a monthly salary of $1,200, the agency fee may be from 75 percent to 100 percent of that, or $900 to $1,200. Other agencies charge a flat rate regardless of the salary. Some agencies include a detailed background check in their fee, while others charge extra for this service. In addition, more agencies are now charging parents a nonrefundable application fee, which may or may not be applied to the placement fee.

Nanny Agency Guarantees

While almost all agencies offer some sort of a guarantee regarding their services, what they offer varies greatly.

Only rarely will an agency refund any portion of your fee if a nanny leaves your employ prior to the end of the guarantee period. Most agencies claim that they will make every effort to find a replacement nanny for you at no additional cost, for a limited period of time—usually 30, 60, or 90 days. But if a nanny leaves and the agency sends replacements for you to interview, you may not like any of the other nannies. You then are faced with hiring a nanny you wouldn't have hired in the first place or starting over with another agency, paying another fee, and hoping for a better nanny.

Try to negotiate with the agency on your payment of its fee. The agency may let you make three installment payments over the period of your guarantee, to ensure that you aren't out the whole $1,200 fee and left without a nanny.

Questions to Ask Nanny Agencies

How long have you been in business?

Most agencies close after one or two years in business. The longer an agency has been operating, the better the odds that it is meeting the needs of parents.

What is the background of the person who will be selecting the nannies I will interview?

Many agencies are operated by a single individual, and it is important to know what skills this person has—in other words, what qualifies this person to make such an important decision on your behalf. A background in human resources or perhaps child development would better enable the person to assess a nanny's skill level and suitability for your position.

What is your philosophy for matching nannies with families?

An agency should be able to describe a formula that it uses to successfully match candidates with families. This formula should include more than just that the nanny is seeking a full-time live-in position and you happen to have a full-time live-in job available. The agency should delve into the nanny's background, hobbies, and interests—and it should ask you to define your family's personality so that it can find the best fit.

To what degree do you investigate a nanny's background? How many work references and personal references do you require? Do I have access to the nanny's complete record on file with you, including documentation of her work references?

A nanny agency should be able to provide you with at least two child care references—not from relatives—for a nanny, and preferably three references. You should also request personal references from nonrelatives. Some agencies will say that personal references don't mean anything, but the more people you can reach to verify that this individual is who she says she is, the better.

To what degree do you check for a criminal background?

Some nanny agencies do not check for a criminal background. Some consider a report from the department of motor vehicles (DMV) (an identification verification and a printout of convictions while operating an automobile) to be enough of a clearance. Others will check city or county police records to determine if any police reports were filed on the nanny. But if a nanny has moved around often, a city or county check may not be enough. Look for a nanny agency that does a background check in each county where the nanny has lived or worked.

In California, all nanny agencies are required by law to clear any nanny through the California Trustline Registry, or to have at least started her application through Trustline prior to your hiring her. (Trustline is a state-run program that provides a background check on nanny candidates; see pages 44, 82.) An agency's failure to do this is a misdemeanor. Offering Trustline as an option to parents is not considered compliance. If you are working with a nanny agency in California, demand that this be included in your fee. California is currently the only state to offer such a program, but Trustline is viewed as a model for future programs in other states.

Checklist for Selecting an Agency

☐ Interview all agencies, using the questions above as a guide.

☐ Find out if your state requires nanny agencies or employment agencies to be licensed by contacting your state department of consumer affairs. If so, make sure the agency's license is current. Ask how long ago the license was issued and if it was ever revoked.

☐ If the agency claims any affiliations, verify them. For example, if it claims to be a member of the International Nanny Association (INA), call the INA to verify that its membership is current. Parents have reported agencies that sign on for one year and then continue to advertise that they are members, even though their membership has expired.

☐ Call the Better Business Bureau to find out if any claims were ever filed against the agency. An agency doesn't have to be a member to have claims filed against it.

☐ Ask the agency to provide you with names and addresses of their three most recent clients (within the last 30 days). Ask those parents if they felt they got their money's worth of service from the agency. Make sure the agency doesn't just give you three happy customers. Request the *last three clients* so that you can determine the current level of service. Verify with the parents when they worked with the agency.

If an agency can't answer the questions above or isn't willing to provide you with license numbers, professional affiliations, and at least three current clients you can contact for a reference, that agency should not be your first choice.

Keep in mind that there are good nanny agencies out there. But any good agency will admit that, owing to the lack of regulation in the nanny industry, there are also many unscrupulous agencies. With careful investigation, you can find an agency that is up to your high standards.

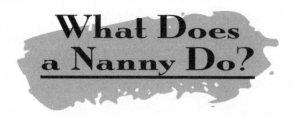

What Does a Nanny Do?

A position as a professional nanny is among the most important jobs one can hold. In addition to providing responsible care, protection, and supervision for "her" children, the professional nanny encourages, teaches, and comforts the children and offers them the love and attention they require, in the absence of their parents, to grow into happy, healthy young people.

The nanny's responsibility to the family includes all aspects of caring for the children, from diapering and feeding to doing their laundry and maintaining their rooms. Just as important is the nurturing of the children. Nannies should plan activities and outings that stimulate children's growth and imagination. Trips to the park, home crafts that are easy and fun, reading time, playtime, and so on—these are all activities the professional nanny should build into the child's day.

In most cases, families ask their nanny to handle routine light housekeeping while the children are napping, such as dusting, vacuuming, and general picking up. Additional housekeeping duties such as family laundry and heavy cleaning are an "extra" and should be discussed with the nanny and agreed upon during the interview process. The nanny should be paid more for these additional duties—$50 to $75 per week extra is the norm.

Usually, the nanny reports for duty early in the morning and is responsible for getting the children up, dressed, and fed. For schoolchildren, she packs lunches and gets them off to school. For younger children, she gets them on with their day. Parents generally return home from work between 5 P.M. and 6 P.M. to relieve the nanny.

A live-in nanny will help prepare dinner and clean up after dinner, just like a member of the family. She should then be free to retire to her room, relax with the family, or go out for the evening. She does not tend to the children in the evening hours unless prior arrangements have been made.

Each morning the nanny and parents should discuss the day ahead—for instance, the parents' schedule, planned activities, and what kind of night the child had. In the evening, the same "changing of the guard" should take place with the nanny reporting back to the parents on the day's events (such as the child's mood, eating habits, discipline problems, and activities). A *Nanny Daily Reporting Log* for this purpose is included later in this book (page 64).

Nannies are typically paid weekly or—if this is agreed to in advance—according to the parents' pay schedule.

Laying the Foundation

Job Description

Before hiring an employee, any business prepares a job description—a detailed list of duties, responsibilities, and requirements. You should do this, too.

The first step in finding the right nanny for your family is to decide what you *want* in a nanny. Prepare a list of functions that the nanny will have to perform, and then list the requirements or skills necessary to perform each function. For instance, is your nanny going to have to drive the children to school, soccer practice, and doctors' appointments? If so, driving should be listed as one function, and one requirement for performing that function will be a driver's license. Another requirement will be a clean report from the DMV. Perhaps the nanny will also need to provide her own car. If so, does she have current insurance, adequate for your children? Does her car have seat belts? Is it in good condition? All these points should be considered necessary requirements or skills related to the function of driving.

Do you have a backyard pool or spa? The nanny will be required to supervise children in your yard, so you will list pool supervision as a function. The skills required here include CPR certification. Do you require a nonsmoker? An English-speaker? Certainly, if your nanny is to care for an infant, one requirement would be prior experience with infants.

Think ahead about your needs, and write them down. The nanny who seems most personable during an interview can become a disaster if you find out too late that she is a chain-smoker or has a poor driving record.

A job description, then, helps you keep your focus (it's very easy to get distracted when Mary Poppins shows up at your door). In addition, a written job description prepared in advance will help you in the screening process. You can verify your basic requirements over the phone when a candidate responds to your ad, even before she completes an application, saving yourself hours of "courtesy" interviewing.

Salary

Nannies' salaries vary greatly from region to region. In the northeast, nannies are often paid $400 to $500 or more per week. In California, however, the average nanny's weekly salary is closer to $300 to $350 per week. Within southern California, wages are higher in Los Angeles County than in Orange County or San Diego County, probably because Orange and San Diego counties are close to the Mexican border and a large number of illegal immigrants are seeking domestic work and will accept a lower salary. To determine a competitive rate of pay for your area, contact local nanny agencies for information. Look at the classified ads for domestic help in major newspapers in your area to see what other families are offering.

There are several considerations that will help you determine what to pay your nanny. The primary ones are these:

- Will she live in (with you) or live out (commute)?

- How many children will she care for?

- Will she have other responsibilities in addition to caring for the children?

- How many hours per week will she be required to work?

- Are you offering any benefits in addition to her salary (such as a paid vacation, travel, a cash bonus, or use of the family car)?

Live-In Versus Live-Out

Having a live-in nanny is a dream come true for some families. The nanny tends to become a part of the family, sharing meals and joining in family outings. In some cases, offering live-in accommodations increases the chance that a nanny will stay on for the long term. In addition to offering her employment, you are providing a home and a family. The advantages are considerable for you as well. Because she is always there, you can make a quick trip to the store or out to dinner without having to make special arrangements. Keep in mind, though, that the nanny also needs time for herself to pursue her own interests and be with her own friends. It is essential to establish regular working hours. Any hours above and beyond should be compensated either in cash or in time off.

Live-in accommodations (room and board) are considered part of the nanny's compensation, and therefore the actual amount paid to her can be reduced. For a family that has an extra room and does not require a great deal of privacy, this is an attractive option. In most cases, the nanny has her own room and bath. Sometimes she shares a bath with the children.

Hint: Installing her own phone line with a clear understanding that she is responsible for the bill will go a long way toward preserving a good relationship.

Live-out nannies are generally paid $75 to $100 per week more than those who live in. A live-out nanny has to contend with the commute each day, and she can put you behind schedule if she arrives at work late; but having her leave at the end of the day gives you both your own "space" and a chance to regenerate. Sometimes that is the key to long-term commitment.

How Many Children Will the Nanny Care For?

Day care centers charge full tuition for each child, though some do offer a minimal discount for more than one child per family. Nannies, by contrast, are usually paid the same rate for up to three children and then compensated nominally for each additional child. For example, a live-in nanny caring for one or two children might be paid an average of $300 per week, depending on her responsibilities, her experience, and so on. For the same situation with a third or fourth child, the nanny is usually paid an extra $10 to $20 per child per week.

For parents who have twins, it is a blessing to find a nanny with experience caring for infant twins. Usually a nanny will care for two children near the same age without requesting a higher rate of pay. However, offering more money to a nanny with such experience may be necessary in order to make your position more desirable than another position she may be considering. The extra money you pay her may well be worth it to obtain her services.

Nanny Sharing

One way to attract a highly qualified nanny and still stay within your budget is to share a nanny. If two families have one child each and they live in close proximity to one another, sharing a nanny is one way to get a high-caliber nanny at half the price. If each family pays $150 per week, resulting in a salary of $300 per week for the nanny, everyone is benefiting! The downside to this scenario is that if one family pulls out of the partnership, the other family is left to either the full salary of $300 per week (the nanny will not want to take a cut in pay) or look for a new nanny. Each family must be committed in order for this arrangement to work.

Additional Responsibilities

Will the nanny be required to maintain the house? Routine dusting and vacuuming are usually responsibilities the nanny will agree to handle during the day's quiet time. Beyond that, she should be compensated for housekeeping responsibilities. Cleaning baths, showers, and the kitchen; shopping for groceries; cooking; and, especially, doing the family laundry are all considered above and beyond the duties of a professional nanny. Keep in mind that, depending on the ages of your children, extra duties will take the nanny's attention away from them. She may be inclined to make household chores a priority because not doing them will be more noticeable to you than not reading or playing with your little ones—the primary reason you hired her in the first place.

Hours

Most parents require that their nanny be ready to take charge between 6:30 A.M. and 7:30 A.M. if they themselves have the usual eight- or nine-to-five jobs. This allows the nanny to care for the children while the parents dress and get on their way to work. The nanny prepares breakfast, packs school lunches, and gets the children off to school. If the children are younger, she gets their day started at home.

Whether the nanny lives in or out, her workday should end when the parents return home. If she is asked to start dinner, the parents should take over the preparation when they have settled in, generally about 6 P.M. Remember, this is almost a 12-hour day for the nanny. True, there is downtime when the children are sleeping, but the nanny is still on call and cannot leave. In effect, she is on duty the entire 12 hours.

Try to adhere to an agreed-upon schedule. Just as you expect to be able to leave your job at a specific time, so too your nanny needs to be confident that you will not take advantage of her.

Benefits

A business offers benefits to attract and retain high-caliber employees, and many parents are now offering benefits to make a position desirable and to keep the nanny on the job longer. According to the International Nanny Association, there are many more families seeking nannies than qualified nannies available. It may be necessary to offer more than just a good salary in order to attract a high-quality nanny. There are a variety of options available to you, some at no cost, that add to the nanny's overall compensation package.

One benefit that costs you nothing but might be very valuable to your nanny is the *option of bringing her own child to work with her.* This allows her to be with her child and saves her the cost of child care. While this may seem contrary to the whole point of individualized care, the arrangement has worked well for many families. The nanny is often happier; your child, if a preschooler, has a playmate, and thus gets the kind of socialization a preschool offers; and your chances of retaining the nanny are greater. This is a real bonus for nannies, though admittedly it works for some families and not for others.

Vacations are another benefit to be considered. This should be presented to the candidates at the time you are interviewing them. Will your nanny receive a paid vacation each year when you take yours? Perhaps you will take her along with you, paying her way? These are benefits that make a good nanny want to work for you, rather than another family she may be considering.

Bonuses are also a good incentive. Consider offering a bonus to your nanny every six months or every year. Explain at the outset that the bonus will be paid after she has shown you that she is doing her very best for your child. Her ability to nurture your children, plan interesting activities and projects with them, and provide those hugs and kisses will all be factors that affect the bonus. Again, this serves as an incentive for the nanny to stay on with you. She has a financial interest in doing so. A cash bonus is always appreciated, but a restaurant certificate, a gift certificate to her favorite store, or even a few extra days off (perhaps Grandma might watch the children) are ways to reward her for a job well done.

Use of the family car is another way to make your offer more attractive than the Joneses' offer. Allowing your live-in nanny to use your car in the evenings and on weekends will save her money on car payments, maintenance, and insurance. Provided that your own insurance is adequate to cover her as a driver, this is a great benefit at little or no additional cost to you.

Medical insurance is high on the "want list" for most nannies. Group insurance rates are available for nannies through the International Nanny Association. As of this printing, Richard A. Eisenberg Associates is the official insurance representative of the INA. You can get more information by dialing (800) 777-5765. This firm offers nannies (and families) life insurance, health insurance, disability insurance, and investment plans. Contact Eisenberg for an information packet to show your candidates at the time of the interview. Explain that after six months you will consider paying for her insurance (or sharing the cost) if you feel she is doing her best for your child.

A healthy, happy nanny will ultimately benefit your own children.

Other Considerations for Hiring

Age

Before you make your final decision, consider what is the best age for your child's nanny. Are you looking for the "grandmotherly" type with years of experience, who will spend lots of time reading to your children and will encourage them in a quiet way? Or do you require a "high-energy" nanny who can keep up with little Junior?

Don't eliminate a candidate because of age (there are a lot of grandmothers out there with more energy than new mothers), but do be clear during the interview about what is required. If the nanny is to carry a toddler up the stairs several times a day for diaper changing, an older candidate may tire too easily. If the nanny is expected to engage in physical activities like playing ball with the children, taking trips to the beach, or supervising backyard swimming, make sure she is capable of such activities. An older nanny who isn't interested in such an "active" role will probably tell you that this isn't the job for her. If there are other household chores included in her job description, assess whether the nanny is able to handle them physically. Hiring a nanny only to find out that she can't keep up with your family can be a real disappointment and may require that you begin your search all over again.

Style

Style is something else to think about. This is a different concern from energy level. Does the candidate appear to be the type who will get right in there with the children, playing along with them, or does she appear to be just a supervisor? Is she a real nurturer or just a diaper-changer? During your interview, try to determine her style by asking appropriate questions (see "The Interview" page 31).

Having considered the preceding questions, you now have a firm foundation upon which to begin your search. You have carefully considered the type of person you desire, the experience you require, the salary you will pay, the benefits you will offer, and the specific duties you expect your nanny to perform. Had you not carefully considered these issues, you would be proceeding without any focus, rethinking each step of the way, and possibly compromising and lowering your standards.

You are now focused, prepared, and ready for the next step.

Nanny Job Description

On page 19 you will find a form for a *Nanny Job Description.* This form should be completed by you and then copied as many times as necessary and given to candidates at the time they complete the application form. (More on the application form and process later.)

Putting in writing what is required and expected, from the start, will eliminate confusion and problems down the road.

The
Nanny
Kit

Nanny Job Description

Family Name _____

Address _____

_____

Telephone _____

We are seeking a nanny to work: ❑ Full-time   ❑ Part-time

The position available is for: ❑ Live-in   ❑ Live-out

The days and hours our nanny will be required to work are:

Sunday _____ Monday _____ Tuesday _____ Wednesday _____ Thursday _____ Friday _____ Saturday _____

Our nanny will be responsible for the following children:

Name _____ Sex _____ Age _____   Name _____ Sex _____ Age _____

Name _____ Sex _____ Age _____   Name _____ Sex _____ Age _____

Child care responsibilities include:

❑ Infant care   ❑ Bathing   ❑ Children's rooms   ❑ Outside play   ❑ Driving children

❑ Meal preparation   ❑ Children's laundry   ❑ Giving medication   ❑ Reading/activities   ❑ Homework help

Additional responsibilities:

❑ Dusting   ❑ Ironing   ❑ Shopping   ❑ Vacuuming   ❑ General pickup

❑ Cooking   ❑ Family laundry   ❑ Cleaning bathrooms   ❑ Errands

---

Requirements for the position:

❑ Child care experience   ❑ Infant care experience   ❑ CPR certificate   ❑ Own car and insurance   ❑ High school graduate

❑ Nonsmoker   ❑ English-speaker   ❑ English-reader/writer   ❑ Verifiable references

❑ Early childhood training   ❑ Other _____

You must be willing to provide and/or authorize:

❑ Written application   ❑ DMV report   ❑ Medical clearance   ❑ Fingerprints   ❑ Proof of CPR

❑ TB test   ❑ Proof of insurance   ❑ Background investigation

Comments _____

_____

_____

Recruiting Your Nanny

Strategies for Recruiting

There are several avenues you can take in recruiting a nanny. If time is a concern, advertising in your local paper is probably your best bet. A well-worded classified ad is a good beginning, but there are other strategies as well.

Consider a *job posting in the child development center* of your local college. You will be reaching people who are genuinely interested (and presumably educated) in this field. Chances are, this is a career they are considering as well.

If you are seeking after-school care only, local colleges are an ideal place to recruit because many college students attend only morning classes. An *ad in the college newspaper* and *postings on bulletin boards on campus are ideas.*

Don't discount the loving care of seniors! Grandmotherly types (this author's personal preference) can be found by *advertising in senior publications* and *posting cards at senior centers.*

An ad on the *bulletin board at work* may also be a good place to recruit. Perhaps someone you know may have a daughter or an aunt looking for a child care position. You might even come across people who no longer need their own nanny and would love to help her find a position.

Perhaps the best resource available is another nanny in your neighborhood. Very often, nannies network with each other and are aware of family or friends who are looking for work. (However, just the fact that you get a referral from someone who has a family member willing to work doesn't mean you need to do any less in the way of checking on her background.)

You might even *contact your local day care centers for leads*. Reassure the director that you are not seeking to steal any of the center's employees, but ask if she knows qualified applicants who she doesn't have positions for. Tell her that you will be happy to make a contribution to the school's fund-raising efforts, purchase a new set of books for its library, or even offer the director herself a gift certificate if she is able to refer a candidate to you that you ultimately hire. Caregivers who apply to work in commercial day care centers usually have a certain level of skills and education, and their background information may be prepared. They already have their TB test results, their DMV report, and their fingerprints ready, and they may also have earned early childhood education units through a local college. The caliber of such a caregiver may be higher than that of an individual answering your newspaper ad.

Writing the Ad

Write the kind of ad that will attract the nanny you are looking for. The more specific you are in the ad, the better the odds of weeding out less desirable candidates. A few extra dollars spent on a well-worded ad can save you lots of time in the screening process.

When you write the ad, picture the nanny reading it. It is her first impression of you and your family, and it will help set the tone for your relationship.

A typical ad reads:

> **Live-in for 3 yrs and infant. Lght hskpng, ref req. Call eve. 555-1234**

A more effective ad for the same position would read:

> **Live-in nanny to nurture and care for our energetic 3-yr-old son and infant daughter. Experience with infants and excellent references required. Nonsmoker, CPR certified, excellent driver. Offering own room and bath, good salary. Be a part of our family. 555-1234.**

This ad implies that you are not looking for just anyone. It says that you expect more and are prepared to offer more in return. It is clear that the nanny must be a good driver and CPR certified, for instance. You can hope that anyone who lacks these credentials will not call to inquire. If unqualified candidates do call, simply explain that in order to be interviewed, they must meet your minimum requirements.

If you are placing your ad in the newspaper, carefully select the heading under which it will appear. The larger papers not only have an employment section but also have a special section, "Domestic Employment," that appears after the regular help-wanted ads. Some papers even break the domestic listings down into nannies, companions, live-ins, and housekeepers.

Telephone Screening

 If properly conducted, screening by telephone will save you untold hours of time and frustration. Keep the *Nanny Phone Screening Log* (page 24) near your telephone to record data on each caller.

A NOTE ON TIMING

There is a tendency to want to hire the first person who seems right for the position, particularly if time is a concern for you. While you don't want to lose a candidate to another family because you are dragging your feet, neither do you want to hire too hastily, lest the truly perfect nanny show up at your door the next day. Give yourself and your candidates a time frame for hiring. Let everyone who applied know that you are interviewing through the end of the week, for instance, and that you will be making a decision the following week after verifying references.

Here are some questions for telephone screening:

1. Ask for the nanny's name, address, and phone number. (You may note right away that the city or neighborhood she lives in is not close enough to be practical.)

2. Ask if she meets all the requirements listed in the ad.

3. How does she sound over the phone? (For instance: sincere, youthful, mature, professional?)

4. Is she currently interviewing? Does she have offers pending? (This will give you an idea of the "marketability" of the caller. Is she "in demand"?)

5. Briefly explain the hours, duties, and salary, and ask if these are acceptable to her.

A NOTE ON TAXES

The Nanny Kit assumes that both the parents and the nanny plan to report income and pay the required "nanny tax." But the author recognizes that less than half of parents and nannies actually comply with this requirement. Therefore, it's a good idea to ask your nanny candidate if she is willing to have her wages reported (so that you can claim a child care credit on your taxes) and to share the payment of her social security contribution (see "Social Security Tax," page 54). Determine whether the salary she is requesting is pretax. She may be thinking that the amount you agree to pay is what she will net *after* deductions are taken out. Often, parents neglect to ask this up front and find out all too late that they and the nanny have totally different ideas about the amount of money that she will take home at the end of the week.

If everything checks out during this brief phone conversation, tell the candidate that you will send out an application form (see page 25). Include a copy of your *Nanny Job Description*. Ask her to complete the application and return it to you immediately. You should include a self-addressed, stamped envelope to expedite return.

Expect to receive less than half of the applications you send out. Only those candidates who are truly interested and qualified will return an application to you. Don't be discouraged—you didn't want the others anyway. The application itself is essential to obtaining important information about the nanny. Should a problem occur, you will have a record of previous addresses, other names used, previous employers, and more.

Nanny Application Form

A detailed application is the beginning of the employment process for any job, including file clerk, mailroom monitor, or floor sweeper. Anyone who becomes defensive about providing the information requested is suspect and not the person to care for your child.

Copy the *Nanny Application* form (page 25) as many times as necessary. It includes all the information you will need to verify the candidate's experience, references, citizenship, and health.

Most important, this application will serve as a guide for the interview itself.

Nanny Phone Screening Log

Date of Call	Nanny's Name	Address/Phone	Date Application Sent	Comments

Nanny Application

Please answer all questions completely, including full names, addresses, phone numbers, and dates. All the information provided will be verified.

Full name _____
   First   Middle   Last

Maiden name or other names used _____

Address _____
   Street   City/State   Zip

   *How long at the above address?*_____

Previous address _____
   Street   City/State   Zip

   *How long at the previous address?*_____

Telephone number (_____)_____   Message number (_____) _____

Emergency contact name _____   Relationship_____

   Address _____

   Phone number (_____)_____

What kind of position are you seeking?   ❏ Full-time   ❏ Part-time

                                                  ❏ Live-in   ❏ Live-out

Please indicate the days and hours you are available to work:

Sunday _____   Monday _____   Tuesday _____   Wednesday _____   Thursday _____   Friday _____   Saturday _____

Are you a U.S. citizen?   Yes ❏   No ❏

Social Security #: _____   Green card or work authorization identification #: _____

Driver's license #: _____   Driver's license expiration date : _____

(Note: I-9 Form required)

Do you speak English?	❏ Yes	❏ No
Do you read English?	❏ Yes	❏ No
Do you write English?	❏ Yes	❏ No

List any other languages you speak: _____

Are you 18 years old or older?	❏ Yes	❏ No
Are you a high school graduate?	❏ Yes	❏ No

Name of high school: _____   Year graduated: _____

EMPLOYMENT HISTORY   Please list the last five positions you have held and account for all periods of unemployment.

Employer _____

Address _____
            Street   *City/State*   *Zip*

Phone (____)_____

Dates of employment _____ *to* _____

Duties (if child care, list ages of children and duties):

Reason for leaving:

Rate of pay:

Employer _____

Address _____
            Street   *City/State*   *Zip*

Phone (____)_____

Dates of employment _____ *to* _____

Duties (if child care, list ages of children and duties):

Reason for leaving:

Rate of pay:

Employer _____

Address _____
            Street   *City/State*   *Zip*

Phone (____)_____

Dates of employment _____ *to* _____

Duties (if child care, list ages of children and duties):

Reason for leaving:

Rate of pay:

EMPLOYMENT HISTORY–Continued

Employer _____

Address _____
  Street   City/State   Zip

Phone (____)_____

Dates of employment _____ *to* _____

Duties (if child care, list ages of children and duties):

Reason for leaving:

Rate of pay:

Employer _____

Address _____
  Street   City/State   Zip

Phone (____)_____

Dates of employment _____ *to* _____

Duties (if child care, list ages of children and duties):

Reason for leaving:

Rate of pay:

Employer _____

Address _____
  Street   City/State   Zip

Phone (____)_____

Dates of employment _____ *to* _____

Duties (if child care, list ages of children and duties):

Reason for leaving:

Rate of pay:

Do you have your own transportation to work?   ❏   Yes   ❏   No

If not, how do you plan to get to and from work each day? _____

Do you smoke?   ❏   Yes   ❏   No

Are you allergic to any pets?   ❏   Yes   ❏   No   Please list_____

Are you currently taking any medication?   ❏   Yes   ❏   No   Please list_____

What do you enjoy doing in your free time?

_____

_____

_____

Why have you chosen to be a nanny?

_____

_____

_____

Please list three personal references (do not include relatives):

Name_____ Relationship_____ Phone (_____)_____

Name_____ Relationship_____ Phone (_____)_____

Name_____ Relationship_____ Phone (_____)_____

Do you agree to provide and/or authorize the following?

Copy of driver's license   ❏   Yes   ❏   No

DMV record check   ❏   Yes   ❏   No

Fingerprints—background check   ❏   Yes   ❏   No

TB test—medical clearance   ❏   Yes   ❏   No

Copy of Social Security card   ❏   Yes   ❏   No

Employment references   ❏   Yes   ❏   No

I verify that the above information is true and accurate to the best of my knowledge. I authorize you to conduct a background check to include past employers, criminal background check, personal references, and the items listed above.

_____   _____

Signature of nanny candidate   Date

Reviewing the Application

Consider how neatly the application has been completed. Have all the questions been answered completely, or has the candidate been vague? If speaking, reading, or writing English is required, does it appear that the nanny understood all the questions and answered appropriately? Has she accounted for all periods of unemployment or breaks between jobs? While this is not likely, a prison term, a hospital stay, or some other undesirable information may be hidden from you simply by omission. Make a note on the application to ask the candidate to explain what she was doing during these breaks in employment. You'll hope that a semester at school or time off to help a sick family member will be the response.

Remember, you have a right to ask almost anything of the nanny. After all, she is going to be caring for the most important people in your life! Anyone who is vague or objects to your questions is not the right person for you.

Parents are often concerned about asking questions that may result in a claim of discrimination. The Equal Employment Opportunities Commission (EEOC) explains that the rules that apply to "employers" are usually different from the rules that apply to "domestic employers." The EEOC will accept claims against employers who employ fifteen or more employees on the standard charges of discrimination by race, national origin, color, religion, age, sex, and physical disabilities. The Department of Fair Employment and Housing will hear claims against employers with five or more employees. So, if you have a nanny, a maid, a chauffeur, a butler, and a cook, you may have to be more careful. The EEOC does point out that a nanny who feels that she was discriminated against can sue you for discrimination in a civil court.

Check that all the reference information is complete. Does the applicant have previous child care experience? How much? How long did she stay with her previous employers? Is she willing to provide a DMV report and a health statement and submit to a background check?

Assuming that you receive many applications, you should assign a numerical rating to each one. Assign points to each candidate based on the following criteria:

1–5 points	Does she meet the skill requirements (experience, certifications, language)?
1–5 points	Rate the employment history (steady employment, longevity).
1–5 points	Rate level of actual experience (previous nanny positions, number of children).
1–5 points	Is the salary requested within your range?

Once you have rated the applications, call back the two or three top-scoring candidates to set up interviews. Some candidates express themselves better over the phone; some express themselves better on paper. Your first impression may change altogether in a face-to-face meeting.

The Interview

Setting Up the Interview

Call each candidate and tell her that you were very impressed with her application and would like to meet her in person to talk. Explain that you are interviewing several candidates and that you hope to make a decision shortly after the interviews and the reference-checking process.

Tell each nanny candidate that you would like to verify everything she listed on the application: ". . . so please bring your driver's license, your Social Security card, your CPR certification, and any written references."

Conducting an Interview

Typically, an interview is a somewhat tense affair for both parties. Follow these tips for a cordial yet professional interview that will help you gain insight into the character, style, temperament, and qualifications of the prospective nanny.

It is recommended that, however endearing they may be, the children *not* be present during the initial interview, so that you don't have any distractions. Some people feel that you must see how the children interact with the nanny, but such a "test" is more appropriate for a second interview. There is so much that you need to find out about *her* first. It's necessary to give your undivided attention to the nanny. It would be appropriate to invite the nanny back for a second interview and at that time introduce the children to her.

Some parents prefer to meet the nanny initially at a "neutral" site, such as a coffeehouse or even at the office. Then, if you are comfortable with her, you can invite her to your home for a second interview and to meet the family.

Remember to ask as many "open-ended" questions as possible—questions that require more than a "yes" or "no" answer. For example, ask the nanny, "What kind of activities do you enjoy doing with children?" This will force her to give you a more thoughtful and insightful answer. Had you asked, "Do you like to read to children?" her answer might be as simple as "yes." You won't gather much information with yes or no questions.

Interview Guidelines

Icebreakers

Greet all candidates warmly. Ask if they found your meeting place easily. A subtle question like, "How long did it take for you to get here?" is an inconspicuous way to gauge a candidate's ability to be punctual. Did she take a bus? What if she missed her bus? These are all points for you to consider.

Setting the Ground Rules

State your case up front. Let the nanny know that you are looking for the best possible care for your children, so you'll be asking a lot of questions that appear probing. Actually, they are probing, but for good reason. Again, a good nanny will understand.

Reviewing the Application with the Nanny

Review each of the points on the application verbally, confirming each one. For example, "So you've lived in this area for the last eight years. Where are you from originally?" Allow the nanny to talk as much as possible. She will give you a wealth of information if you allow her to go on. Suppress the urge to talk about your family. Your objective in this interview is to find out as much as possible about *her*.

Asking About Employment

Discuss each previous employer, starting with the most recent. Questions like "How old were the children you cared for?" and "What were your responsibilities?" will create a dialogue and provide perspective on the nanny.

Always ask why each job came to an end. Was there a personality clash? Always be sympathetic to the nanny, whether or not you agree. Agreeing by nodding your head will encourage her to be open and continue to give you more information on which to form an opinion. Once you become judgmental, she will not be as free with her information.

Asking Hypothetical Questions

Ask thoughtful questions that will help determine the nanny's ability to care for your children. Ask questions such as "How would you handle a fussy baby?" Follow up with other emergency situations: fire, drowning, choking.

Ask how she handles a difficult child. How would she prefer to discipline a child if she had her choice? Listen to her response first, then you can share your feelings.

Discussing the Job

Show the candidate the written job description again. Discuss the responsibilities she will have, the hours, and the rate of pay. If she is to live in, explain her accommodations. The second interview is the time to show which bedroom will be hers and which bathroom she will use. Answer any questions she may have honestly.

Sample Interview Questions

Question	What You'll Find Out
About Her . . .	
"Where are you from originally?"	(Where she has been.)
"What brought you here?"	(What she may be leaving behind.)
"How do you like it here?"	(Is she happy here, and how long will she stay?)

About the Profession . . .

Why have you chosen to be a nanny?   (Why not work with adults?)

If her response is "I love children." Ask . . .

"Why not work at a day care center where   (Is she avoiding having supervisors?)
   you're surrounded by children?"

About Previous Employment . . .

"Tell me about the children on your   (Are you comfortable with her
   last job. What were they like?"   response?)
"Have you ever had charge of a difficult   (How will she handle my child?)
   child?"
"Tell me about the parents you worked   (Will we work well together?)
   for. What did you like and not like
   about them?"
"Why did you leave each job?"   (Verify this with her previous em-
                                                        ployers.)

Hypothetical Questions

"You've been on the job for six hours with my colicky baby. She hasn't stopped crying. I'm at work and unavailable. What will you do?"

Most new mothers are anxious to hear the answer to this one. There is no set answer. However, if the nanny just stares blankly at you, she probably hasn't had the experience you require. A good answer might be, "Well, first I'd offer a bottle. Then I'd try a
pacifier. Then I'd check the diaper. If that didn't work, I'd put warmer clothes on or perhaps cooler clothes. I'd sing and rock or, if I'd been doing that, I'd stop singing and
rocking."

"You're at the park and it's time to go, but my 2-year-old refuses. What will you do?"

Ideally, the nanny would approach this question positively. Perhaps she'll say
something like, "I would tell him about the next fun thing we are going to do when we

get home to motivate him to come along willingly—such as, 'Let's go home and have a snack!' If he still didn't come, I might say, 'Okay, let's stay for five more minutes and then we have to go.'"

"What is your philosophy of discipline?"

The nanny should indicate that she is willing to follow your instructions to the letter concerning discipline. If she has good experience, she might share with you that she utilizes positive discipline with her charges. Another good question is, "How were you disciplined as a child?"

"What activities will you do with my children to stimulate them?"

The nanny should be full of ideas that are age-appropriate for your children. They should include activities that engage all the senses. A good nanny will also point out that the children need time to just play.

Other Questions to Ask:

More About Her . . .

"What do you like to do in your spare time?"
"What was the last book you read?"
"What TV programs do you enjoy watching?"
"If you won the lottery, what would you do with the money?"

Obtaining a Photograph

It's always a good idea to obtain a clear photograph of the nanny for your records. Now is a good time to take a picture, saying that you want to attach it to her application in order to keep straight all the candidates you are interviewing. This is a nonthreatening way to get a close-up shot of the nanny. In the unlikely event that you would need to provide a description of the nanny to the police, the photo will be a big help.

Ending the Interview

 Finally, ask if she has any questions for you. A good nanny might want to know how many nannies *you* have had in the last five years and why each one left. She may ask how long *you* have been on the job, since—after all—her employment depends on *your* stability. The more questions she has, the better the chance that she is seeking a long-term position that is right for her and not just a job to pay the bills.

Explain that you have two other candidates to interview, even if you don't, but that you are interested in her. Verify all the previous employment and reference phone numbers on the application and tell her that you will be back in touch with her shortly for a follow-up interview, to meet the children, and to answer any new questions she might have.

Finally, ask that in the meantime she obtain a TB test (required of all state-licensed caregivers), a DMV report (a record of her driving and an identification verification), and a set of fingerprints (for a criminal check). All these will be explained in detail in the next chapter. Some parents tell the nanny candidate that if she is hired, she will be reimbursed for these expenses. If not, though, she will probably be asked to present them in a future interview.

If she resists on any issue, you may have reason to doubt that she is the right nanny for your family. The owner of a nanny agency in California claims that only 25 percent of nannies who inquire about positions with her agency actually show up for their appointments after they are told they will need to provide this information. That's something to think about.

Nanny Interview Rating Form

 Use the *Nanny Interview Rating* form (see page 37) to assess each candidate immediately after the interview. By assigning a numerical value to each person interviewed, you will have a more objective assessment of her abilities and qualifications for the position. Of course, your gut feeling does account for something. However, using a rating system ensures that you have evaluated each nanny on all the key issues you laid out at the beginning of your search.

Nanny Interview Rating

Immediately after each nanny leaves the interview, rate her on each of the following questions, using a scale from 1–5 (5 being the highest). Total her points at the bottom of the page, and you will have an objective evaluation of the candidates.

Name of nanny _____

_____ First impression of the nanny?

_____ Level of child care experience?

_____ Level of additional skills?

_____ How steady is her employment history?

_____ Does her age or style mirror your requirements?

_____ Does her philosophy of discipline mirror your own?

_____ Does she seem likely to truly "nurture" your child?

_____ Is she enthusiastic about being a nanny?

_____ Will she be able to keep up with your busy children?

_____ How well will she react in an emergency?

_____ Is she agreeable to any additional household duties?

_____ Will she fit in well with your family?

_____ Overall impression of her?

_____ **Total points earned**

The Background Check

Conducting a Reference Check

Use the reference check forms (see pages 41 and 42) to verify all the information on the application as well as that obtained in the interview.

Begin with the candidate you are most interested in, but try to juggle a second-choice candidate, too. Everything may check out well on your first choice when suddenly something like a conviction for drunk driving appears that would eliminate her as a contender.

The information you obtain from previous employers is most important, so be clear in your questioning. The questions below will help you obtain a good picture of your prospective nanny's previous employment.

When you call a reference, consider that you are calling unannounced. Ask, "Is this a good time?" If not, call back at an agreed-upon time. Try to "partner" the person by explaining that you are a concerned parent and want to make the best decision for your children and that you would appreciate candid answers to your questions.

1. **Verify the employment dates** the nanny gave you and make sure they match with the employer's recollection. Try to get the employer to give you the information, rather than asking the parent to confirm the dates you have. For example, ask, "What period of time did she work for you?" Let the reference tell you the dates. If you were to say, "She said she worked from January to June of 1997. Is that correct?" you might open the door to a fraudulent reference.

2. **Verify the salary she was paid and the duties she performed.** A discrepancy in salary claimed or duties performed is a red flag. It is imperative that you maintain an honest relationship with your nanny on all counts, right from the beginning.

3. **"On a scale of 1 to 10—10 being best—how would you rate her?"** If the rating is not a 10, ask, "Why not a 10?" This will help the reference to pinpoint any flaws.

4. **Why did she leave your employ?** Remember to ask the reference "why." Do *not* ask the reference to confirm what the nanny told you—again, you could become vulnerable to a fraudulent reference.

5. **Would you rehire her?**

6. **Did your children like and respect her?**

7. **What were her best qualities and her weaknesses?**

8. **"She will be caring for my children, is there anything else you think I should know?"** One mother asked this question and the other parent reported that the nanny had lied to her! The mother was surprised. "But you gave her a good reference! How could you now tell me that she lied?"

   The parent responded, "She was always on time and took good care of the children. The dates and rate of pay she told you were accurate. My children liked her. However, she would have her boyfriend over, even though I told her visitors were not allowed. I eventually found out that he was visiting during the day and she had lied to me."

   Quite a bit of insight! Had this mother not asked, "Is there anything else you think I should know?" she might not have found this out.

9. **Finally, leave your name and phone number with the other parent.** If the references are reluctant to share something with you, but decide later that they should, they will now have a way to contact you. One mother left her number with the other mother and the next morning received a call back. The woman told her, "You sounded like a concerned mother. After thinking about it all night, I decided to call you back to tell you that there were suspicious bruises on

my child and that's really why we let our nanny go. We had no firm evidence of abuse, so we didn't pursue it. I just thought you should know this."

Chilling, isn't it? Imagine if she hadn't left her phone number. She might never have known.

Nanny Employment Reference Check

Nanny's name _____

Previous employer: Date of call:

Dates of employment: Rate of pay:

If child care, verify ages of children and duties:

Rating on a scale of 1 to 10 (10 being best):   Why did she leave?

Would you rehire her?   Best qualities/Weaknesses?

Comments:

Previous employer: Date of call:

Dates of employment: Rate of pay:

If child care, verify ages of children and duties:

Rating on a scale of 1 to 10 (10 being best):   Why did she leave?

Would you rehire her?   Best qualities/Weaknesses?

Comments:

Previous employer: Date of call:

Dates of employment: Rate of pay:

If child care, verify ages of children and duties:

Rating on a scale of 1 to 10 (10 being best):   Why did she leave?

Would you rehire her?   Best qualities/Weaknesses?

Comments:

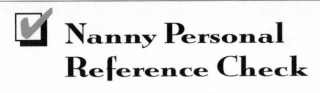

Nanny Personal Reference Check

Nanny's name _____

Personal reference name: Date of call:

How long have you known her?   Where did you meet?

How is she with children?

In what situations have you observed her with children?

Would you recommend her for a nanny position?

She will be caring for my children. Is there anything else you think I should know?

Personal reference name: Date of call:

How long have you known her?   Where did you meet?

How is she with children?

In what situations have you observed her with children?

Would you recommend her for a nanny position?

She will be caring for my children. Is there anything else you think I should know?

Personal reference name: Date of call:

How long have you known her?   Where did you meet?

How is she with children?

In what situations have you observed her with children?

Would you recommend her for a nanny position?

She will be caring for my children. Is there anything else you think I should know?

Testing

Most state-licensed day care centers require certain tests of applicants for teaching and child care positions. A TB test, a DMV report, and fingerprinting are all routine application procedures.

Your home is not licensed, and the caregiver who works in your home is not obligated to be licensed, but this does *not* mean that you should be any less thorough in referencing and testing your nanny. In fact, your nanny will be working in your home unsupervised by a day care center director and other employees; this gives you even more justification for being very complete in your background investigation.

TB Testing

Tuberculosis (TB) screening involves a small pinprick on the surface of the skin. The nanny may go to her own doctor, to your family doctor, or to a clinic to have the test performed. After three days, the skin's appearance is examined to determine whether the nanny is a carrier of the disease. The nanny may have a positive TB test, indicating that she is a *carrier* of the disease, but a chest X ray may show that she is not *infected* with the disease. Tuberculosis can be dormant for years in an individual who may never develop the disease. For others, the disease may become active because of diet, stress, and low resistance.

For parents of infants and small children who are still developing their immune systems, this is an issue to discuss seriously with your child's pediatrician.

Remember to allow a few extra days for this test in your overall time frame for hiring. Illegal immigrants to the United States, many of whom have not been immunized according to standards in this country, are one of the largest groups of individuals seeking domestic employment.

It would also be prudent to have the nanny provide a health clearance from her doctor, stating simply that she is in good physical condition and able to care for active youngsters. You may also want to know if she is taking any regular medication, or if she has any medical conditions that would cause her to faint (leaving your child unattended) or that could cause a lapse in memory or judgment. You may write to her doctor requesting these more specific assurances, as long as the nanny has also signed the letter indicating that she authorizes the doctor to release this information.

DMV Report

The department of motor vehicles (DMV) report is another check that provides information on your candidate.

A DMV report will verify her identity, provide any other names she has used, and also list previous addresses. You can compare this with the information she provided on her written application.

The DMV report also lists any traffic convictions that would be important to you (such as drunk driving convictions or multiple speeding tickets). Even if your nanny is not going to be driving your children, the information in the report is valuable in helping you to determine if this person is the right caregiver for you.

In most cases the DMV report costs less than $10. Some states require that the nanny herself must come in person to request the report (this is the case in California). Others allow you to obtain written authorization from the individual whose report you are requesting. Check with your local DMV for its policy.

Fingerprinting

A fingerprint check is another routine procedure in most state-licensed facilities, and it should be included in your battery of tests for prospective nannies.

For about $10, most municipal police departments will take fingerprints of your candidate. They will give the nanny a card with her prints to deliver to you. How do you know these are the prints of the nanny? The police officer taking the prints checks the nanny's photo identification against her signature and then stamps the card, indicating this is the individual whose prints are on the card.

Just having your nanny's fingerprints on record is not enough. You must now contact your state department of justice to determine how to have the prints reviewed. California has established a new organization called the Trustline Registry. Upon receipt of your application, your candidate's fingerprints, and a fee (at the time of this writing, the fee is $90), Trustline will examine the California Criminal Conviction Records and the California Child Abuse Index (for substantiated allegations of child abuse) and verify identification of your candidate through the DMV. If a candidate clears these tests, she will be placed on the registry as a Registered Trustline Child Care Provider. If she is denied clearance, she is notified and has an opportunity to appeal. If a nanny claims to be a Registered Trustline Child Care Provider, Trustline will, at no cost to you, verify this claim in minutes.

All nanny placement agencies in California are required by law to place *only* Trustline-registered nannies. Should you go to an agency in that state, ask whether it is abiding by this law.

Some agencies advertise that their nanny candidates are fingerprinted, meaning merely that the agency has obtained a set of prints for the record. If something should happen, the nanny's prints are on file. This is an after-the-fact measure, not a background check.

Keep in mind that while requesting fingerprints may seem extreme to some people, you are requesting only the same clearance that the state requests of its licensed caregivers. You are leaving your child in the care of this person, who would most likely *not* volunteer a conviction record in an interview.

The nature of domestic employment, and the fact that most parents do little or no investigating, make this an attractive career choice for someone with a less than sterling background.

Verifying CPR Certification

Cardiopulmonary resuscitation (CPR) certification should be required of every parent as well as every caregiver. Anyone to whom a child is entrusted should know how to save that child's life in an emergency. Proof of *current* certification should be provided. A class taken ten years ago is better than no training, but be aware that CPR—particularly infant CPR—has changed dramatically over the years. If your top nanny candidate meets all of your other requirements and is not CPR-certified, request that she take a CPR class as a condition of her employment. If she has a valid CPR certificate, request that she take a refresher class at your expense, prior to starting work. It's a good idea for parents to take this class with the nanny in order to ensure that she is capable of this important lifesaving procedure.

✔ Nanny Verifications

Use this form to make sure you have seen and/or received a copy of each of the following and have verified all claims this nanny has made regarding employment, education, identification, and certifications.

Nanny's name_____

_____ Driver's license (received copy)

_____ Social Security card/work authorization identification (received copy)

_____ Completed I-9 Form (see page 52)

_____ Current CPR certificate (received copy)

_____ DMV report (received copy)

_____ TB test (received copy)

_____ Fingerprints—only originals

_____ Conducted criminal background check (received copy of report from investigation)

_____ Conducted personal reference check

_____ Conducted employment reference check

Comments:

The Offer

Nanny Work Agreement

When you are ready to offer the position to your top nanny candidate, it is important that the offer be complete and in writing. Oral agreements can be misunderstood and can cause conflicts in the future that could result in the loss of your nanny.

Use the *Nanny Work Agreement* form (see page 49) to put into writing everything you are offering your nanny (salary, accommodations, bonuses, and benefits) and all of her duties. Both you and the nanny should sign the agreement. Retain a copy for your files. The nanny should also be given a copy of the signed agreement for her records. Any later changes in your understanding with her should be documented in the form of an amendment.

Ground Rules

Now is the time to discuss the ground rules—the specifics governing your relationship with the nanny that don't go into the work agreement. The following is a list of suggested topics to make clear *before* she begins working:

Absolutes—Causes for Immediate Termination

- Striking the children

- Lying

- Leaving the children unattended

Other Ground Rules

Television	Types of programs and time limits for both children and nanny.
Telephone	Who pays for personal calls? Also: you need the phone clear in case you need to reach her.
Visitors	No one should be in your home unless you have approved in advance.
Visiting	No visiting her friends and family at their homes unless you know in advance and have given permission. When your nanny takes your child to visit friends or family, you have no control over the situation. Who will be there? What will be taking place? Is the nanny's crazy uncle there—someone who might cause harm to your child? Part of the reason you are hiring in-home care for your child is to retain control over the environment. This is a point to consider when your nanny asks about taking your children "out."
Off-Limits	Areas of the home that are off-limits. Your bedroom?
Music	What kind of music do you want your children exposed to? How loud? How long?
Curfew	If your nanny lives in, when do you want her to be home?
Kitchen	When are her kitchen privileges?

Also discuss your preferences regarding discipline, nutritious meals, activities, and schedules. Discussing all these issues *now* is important to getting the relationship off the ground and moving in the right direction. If you wait for a reason to discuss these subjects, the discussion might be perceived as a reprimand rather than instruction.

Nanny Work Agreement

Nanny's name: _____ Family's name: _____

Date of hire: _____

Hiring depends on the following conditions (results of background check, providing records, etc.):

_____

_____

Weekly rate of pay: _____ ❏ By check ❏ In cash

Nanny will be paid: ❏ Weekly ❏ Every two weeks ❏ Monthly

Other: _____

Benefits paid by employer (vacation, sick pay, holiday pay, bonuses, etc.):

Days and hours nanny will be required to work:

Sunday _____ Monday _____ Tuesday _____ Wednesday _____ Thursday _____ Friday _____ Saturday _____

Daily responsibilities relating to the children:

❏ Meals ❏ Bathing ❏ Laundry/ironing

❏ Homework ❏ Driving ❏ Cleaning children's rooms

Other duties:

Additional duties:

❏ Cooking ❏ Shopping ❏ Family laundry

❏ Family ironing ❏ Dusting ❏ Vacuuming

❏ Clean baths ❏ Dishwasher ❏ Errands

Other duties:

Our children's routine goes something like this:

Time   *Activity*

_____   _____

_____   _____

_____   _____

_____   _____

_____   _____

Activities we would like to see you engage our children in on a regular basis (such as reading, singing, music, outdoor play, crafts):

Discipline methods we expect you to adhere to:

If situation is live-in, nanny will be provided with:

❏ Own room   ❏ Own bath   ❏ Bath shared with children

❏ Furniture   ❏ Own TV   ❏ Own telephone line

Responsible for long-distance phone charges: ❏ Nanny   ❏ Parent

Other :

Nanny will be reviewed: ❏ Quarterly   ❏ Semiannually

                        ❏ Annually   Next review date: _____

Comments:

_____   _____
Signature of nanny   Date

_____   _____
Signature of parent   Date

Your Responsibilities as a Domestic Employer

Are You a Domestic Employer?

The Internal Revenue Service (IRS) has outlined parameters to help you to determine whether you qualify as a domestic employer. Most parents who employ nannies in their home fall into this category and thus are legally obligated to meet certain responsibilities.

Briefly, these are the basic "tests" to determine if you are a domestic employer:

1. Does your caregiver work in *your* home?

2. Does she use *your* tools and equipment to perform her job (such as diapers, food, toys, baby cribs, and strollers)?

3. Does she take directions from *you*?

A nanny's job description clearly indicates that she is your employee. If you were taking your child to the home of the caregiver or to a day care center, you would become the "customer" rather than the "employer."

For more detailed information, contact the IRS at (800) TAX-FORM and request publication No. 926, Household Employer's Tax Guide.

Your responsibilities as a domestic employer include:

■ Verifying the applicant's right to work (complete Form I-9)

■ Paying and withholding Social Security tax

■ Purchasing a workers' compensation rider to your homeowner's policy

■ Paying unemployment insurance tax

■ Paying your nanny at least the minimum wage

Verifying the Right to Work

 In 1986, Congress passed the Immigration Reform and Control Act, requiring all employers to verify a candidate's right to work in this country. You are required to obtain an I-9 form for each of your employees to indicate that you have verified his or her status. Section 274-A of this act makes it illegal for an employer to knowingly hire illegal aliens or recruit them for a fee. Those who violate this law are subject to specific civil and criminal penalties, ranging from $250 to $10,000 for each employee. A regular pattern or practice of hiring illegal aliens may result in a fine of $3,000 for each employee and up to six months in prison.

You are required to complete an I-9 form for each employee hired and to retain that form for three years or at least one year after the employee has left your employ.

The following are a few of the acceptable forms authorizing work eligibility:

■ Current foreign passport with unexpired stamp that reads "processed for I-551"

■ Form I-551 or passport I-94, which authorizes eligibility for work

■ Alien Registration Receipt Card No. I-551

■ Temporary Residence Card No. I-668

■ Employment Authorization Card No. I-668A

If an applicant has none of the above documents, she may prove her identity and her eligibility for work with the following:

Proof of Identity

- ▣ State driver's license with photo

- ▣ School ID with photo

- ▣ Voter's registration card

- ▣ U.S. military card

- ▣ Draft record

- ▣ Native American tribal documents

- ▣ Canadian driver's license

Proof of Eligibility for Work

- ▣ Social Security card, unless it states "not authorized for work"

- ▣ Unexpired Reentry Permit No. I-327

- ▣ Unexpired Refugee Travel Document No. I-571

The Immigration and Naturalization Service (INS) recently announced a new "green card," which is intended make it more difficult to create a fraudulent document. The new cards have several holograms and an optical stripe on the back that contains the information about the card holder.

You can request the Handbook for Employers (M-274) from the INS. This publication includes illustrations of the documents listed above. You are not responsible for the authenticity of the documents presented to you. The I-9 form requests your signature indicating that the documents presented to you "appear" to be genuine.

This information is a summary of the information available from the Immigration and Naturalization Service and is intended only to give you an overview of your responsibilities. For details on your specific situation, contact your local INS office.

Domestic employment is a prime market for illegal aliens seeking work. Some parents feel that they are "helping out" a nanny who is trying to earn a living and establish herself in this country. However, for parents who hire illegal employees, there are two critical issues to consider.

First, and most important, a nanny who is in this country illegally and caring for your children may be less likely to call for help in an emergency. If she calls 911 for help, she knows that the "authorities" will come. As a result, her status may be discovered. A nanny training specialist cited an example of an illegal nanny who called 911 and then left the child unattended because she was so fearful of being deported.

Second—and secondary in importance to your child's well-being—is the threat of inquiry from both the INS and the IRS. As already pointed out, it is illegal to hire someone who does not have the legal right to work in the country, and the practice is punishable with a fine. The IRS also keeps a watchful eye, as such an arrangement represents a loss of tax revenue.

Social Security Tax

Every employer is required to pay Social Security taxes for an employee if the employee meets the "test" of earning $1,100 or more per year from that employer. Contact your IRS office, your personal tax consultant, or both about your specific situation.

At the time of this printing, a total of 15.3 percent in taxes must be collected for Social Security and Medicare combined. Social Security taxes total 12.4 percent, with the cost shared equally by employer and employee. The employer must pay 6.2 percent of the nanny's wages to Social Security. For example, if your nanny is paid $100 per week, you must pay an additional $6.20 in Social Security taxes. The nanny must also make a contribution of 6.2 percent from her wages.

The Medicare tax for each employer and employee is 1.45 percent, a total of 2.9 percent.

The 1998 changes to the "nanny tax" law (originally implemented in 1995) require most domestic employers to make quarterly estimated tax payments for household help.

According to the Internal Revenue Service, anyone who owes more than $1,000 in total taxes at year's end will be penalized. With the average tax bill for household help totaling more than $2,000, most parents will be required to make estimated payments.

These payments can most easily be made by having your employer withhold your estimated taxes owed from your paycheck. If you choose, you can instead make quarterly payments using Form 1040-EZ. Nanny taxes are still reported annually with the Schedule H attachment to your annual income tax return.

If you employ a nanny and do not pay the required taxes, you are filing a fraudulent tax return and may be penalized. Again, contact your tax adviser for details.

Workers' Compensation

The law also requires you to purchase a "workers' compensation rider" for your employee. Usually this can be done through your existing homeowner's policy. Your current policy probably has a basic plan for "occasional residence employees" (such as the boy who mows the lawn), but if you have an employee who works more than 20 hours per week on a regular basis, she is considered a "permanent residence employee" or an "in-servant." If this is your situation, you must buy additional coverage in the event that your nanny should be injured on the job.

Usually such a rider costs between $175 and $200 per year. It can go a long way toward protecting both the nanny and your personal assets. One couple found out too late, after their nanny was fired and then filed a claim for a back injury, just how expensive *not* complying with this requirement can be.

Contact your insurance representative for details on your obligations, since requirements vary by state. Your insurer can also give you an estimate of the cost.

Unemployment Tax

If your nanny is paid $1,000 or more in a calendar quarter you are required to pay unemployment tax as specified by the Federal Unemployment Tax Act. You may be required to pay both federal and state unemployment tax, depending on which state you live in. Requirements vary by state, so contact your state's unemployment tax agency.

Your taxes owed are calculated on the first $7,000 in wages and may be reduced by any state unemployment taxes you pay.

You are required to pay the unemployment tax from your own funds and are not to withhold this tax from the nanny's wages.

Minimum Wage

The Fair Labor Standards Act requires an employer to pay a nanny at least the minimum wage. At the time of this printing, the federal minimum wage is set at $5.15 per hour. If your state's minimum wage is higher, the higher wage prevails.

Different rules apply for live-in and live-out nannies. A live-in nanny must be paid straight time (at least minimum wage) for any hours worked, with no overtime requirement. A live-out nanny must be paid time-and-one-half for hours worked over 40 hours in a week, but overtime is not required for more than 8 hours in a single day.

Employee or Independent Contractor?

The IRS has established certain "tests" to help parents determine their nanny's status. Many parents believe that if the nanny elects to call herself an "independent contractor," they are relieved of all their "employer" obligations. Not so. Following are some examples of how a nanny fits into the "employee" category rather than the "independent contractor" category:

- Assistants. An employee works for an employer and personally performs the work. An independent contractor may hire assistants to do the work.

- Set hours. An employee works hours determined by the employer. Independent contractors may set their own hours.

- Payment. An employee is usually paid at set intervals, such as hourly, weekly, or monthly. An independent contractor is usually paid at the time the job is completed.

■ Right to quit. An employee can quit her position at any time. An independent contractor is often contractually obligated to complete the assigned task.

Clearly, then, your nanny is *not* an independent contractor. To further clarify your personal situation, contact your local IRS office and request Form SS-8, Determination of Employee Work Status for Purposes of Federal Employment Taxes and Income Tax Withholding.

Employer Identification Number

You, as an employer, must also obtain an employer identification number. Again, contact the IRS and ask for Form SS-4, Application for Employer Identification Number.

Paying Your Nanny

Once you have determined how much and how often you will pay your nanny, it's important to keep a detailed record of the hours she has worked each day and the wages you have paid. Use the *Nanny Time Sheet* (see page 59) to keep a weekly record for your files. This record should indicate the nanny's starting and ending time each day, as well as document any time off granted to the nanny for personal business, any sick time, and any compensation for extra hours worked. The record should also show exactly what her gross pay for the week was, noting any deductions as well as any added compensation (such as a gasoline allowance, reimbursement for groceries, or bonuses). It's a good idea to ask the nanny to "approve" the time sheet each week by signing it as she receives her paycheck from you. The *Nanny Time Sheet* acts as a payroll stub.

Many parents have reported that a discrepancy between what the nanny believes she is owed and what the parents have paid her has caused a great deal of inconvenience for both parties. After being terminated, one nanny took her previous employers to the labor board, claiming that she had worked overtime hours for which she was never paid. The parents had a difficult time preparing their defense because they didn't have clear documentation of hours worked and wages paid. They felt that the nanny didn't need to be paid for overtime hours because they often arrived home early and let her leave early without a loss of wages—but they couldn't prove this. Scrambling to provide other evidence to refute her claim, they also submitted to the labor board long-distance phone charges for calls the nanny had made from their home while she was working. They were faced not only with payment of the back wages, but also with a stiff financial penalty that accrued for each day the nanny's wages were not paid.

Appearing at a hearing entails confusion, frustration, and time off from work. All this could have been avoided if these parents had maintained accurate weekly time sheets and a payroll log.

 Nanny Time Sheet

Nanny's name: _____

Record for week ending: _____

Day	Starting time	Ending time	Total hours worked	Comments
Sunday				
Monday				
Tuesday				
Wednesday				
Thursday				
Friday				
Saturday				

Total hours worked this week: _____

Gross wages: _____

Additional compensation/reimbursement:

+$_____ for _____
+$_____ for _____

Deductions:

−$_____ for _____
−$_____ for _____

Total wages paid this week: _____

_____   _____
Nanny's approval/acknowledgment of wages paid   Date

The Relationship

 Now that you have found your "Mary Poppins," do all that you can, within reason, to keep her happy. As you have just experienced through your own search for a nanny, finding someone you trust and can depend on is no easy task. Take care of your relationship and nurture your nanny as you would want her to nurture your children.

Problem Areas

 There are several areas to be aware of that can result in tension and discontent. They include the following:

Violating the Work Agreement

Do not assume that just because your nanny has agreed to light housekeeping, she will welcome your request to clean out the refrigerator or to scrub the shower. Once you begin to add to her job description, it's easy to ask "just one more favor." Before you realize it, your nanny has become a housekeeper. She will have realized it long before.

If your original work agreement defined her position as a "nanny," then either hire a housekeeper or a cleaning service or compensate her for the additional duties if she agrees to do them.

Violating the Hours Agreed To

If you require your nanny to be on the job at 7 A.M. and have told her that she will be relieved by 6 P.M., then you are obligated to uphold your commitment to these hours. Your nanny has a private life, too. Her time away from your children is important to her as well as to them.

Should you expect to come home late on a given day, tell your nanny in advance and tell her that you will compensate her, either in additional pay or in time off. Remember to treat her with respect and not to take advantage of her—in the same way you would expect to be treated by your employer. Doing so will have a positive effect on your relationship and ultimately on her relationship with your children.

Concerns About Live-In Nannies

When a nanny lives in, one of the concerns most frequently cited by parents is the use of the telephone. Even a live-out nanny should be instructed at the very beginning of the relationship as to your limits on her use of the telephone. Setting up a separate phone line for a live-in nanny will eliminate the concern that she is taking advantage of your kindness, particularly if she is responsible for the bill.

Privacy is another concern, for both parents and nannies, when a nanny lives in. It's a good idea to discuss privacy issues in advance, rather than waiting until a problem occurs. Tell your nanny how you envision your evenings. Do you want her to spend the evening with the family, or would you like that time just for you, your spouse, and your children? What about weekends? Some nannies go "home" for the weekend, but others consider your home to be their home. Do you want the nanny to be included in your weekend activities, or would you like to see her out pursuing her own interests? Discuss this during the interview first, to make sure you are compatible, and then reinforce your wishes during the agreement.

Your Child's Routine

Discuss with your nanny, in advance, what type of activities or what schedule you would like for your child. If you do not verbalize this at the onset, she has no way of knowing what you are expecting. Put your expectations in writing (on the *Nanny Work Agreement*, page 49) and discuss them with her.

Do you want a full schedule with trips to the park, backyard playtime, reading, and crafts? If so, tell this to the nanny.

Do you want your little one to be rocked to sleep? Your nanny may have a different philosophy. Discuss this with her. She is being paid to carry out your wishes, but unless she knows what they are, she will probably do it her way.

Discussing your wishes *at the start* will be interpreted as instruction. But if you wait until you are displeased, your comments will seem like criticism.

Discipline

 Instruct your nanny as to how you would like her to handle discipline. In most cases, a "time-out" for unruly children is the best method for caregivers. Putting up a chart that rewards good behavior with stars and notes bad behavior with check marks is another way to monitor the children's behavior. It is advisable to tell your nanny explicitly that under no circumstances is she to spank, shake, or strike your child in any way. Do make it clear that she should report any problems to you and that you will support her by handling them when you return home.

Appreciating Your Nanny

Your nanny may not have a master's degree, may not supervise a dozen employees, and may not control a million-dollar budget, but she is responsible for supervising something much more valuable—your children.

Let her know how much you appreciate her good work with your children, how pleased you are with the way she handles them, and how at ease you are at work, knowing that they are in her care.

Remembering her birthday or holidays with special gifts or a cash bonus is a wonderful incentive. Just as you appreciate the positive recognition you receive at work, she, too, will welcome your kind words.

Nanny Daily Reporting Log

Ask your nanny to complete the *Nanny Daily Reporting Log* (see page 64) each and every day, to help you understand the events of the day. Not only does this form give you a perspective on your child's day, it also provides the nanny with a reason to discuss problems with you, particularly discipline problems.

If the nanny notes that the child ate wonderfully at each meal, you will understand if he or she eats lightly at dinner. Had you not known this, you might wonder if your child was not feeling well.

The log also shows your nanny that you expect her to be on top of things. You want to know where she and your child went, what they did, what stories they read, and what songs they sang. "No sitters allowed" is the message relayed by this form.

Nanny Daily Reporting Log

Child's name _____ Date _____

Today's meals—child ate:

	Well	Fair	Not so great
Breakfast _____	❏	❏	❏
Lunch _____	❏	❏	❏
Dinner _____	❏	❏	❏

Diapers/potty times:

Time checked	Wet	Dry	BM
_____	❏	❏	❏
_____	❏	❏	❏
_____	❏	❏	❏
_____	❏	❏	❏
_____	❏	❏	❏
_____			

Medications given:

Name of drug_____Time_____Time_____Time_____

Name of drug_____Time_____Time_____Time_____

Today's mood:

❏ Happy   ❏ Energetic   ❏ Curious   ❏ Mellow

❏ Serious   ❏ Passive   ❏ Tired

Today's activities: _____

Stories we read today: _____

Boo-boo report/first aid: _____

Behavior report: _____

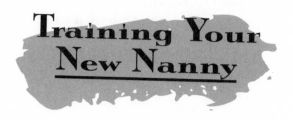

Training Your New Nanny

Okay. Your nanny has passed all your tests, jumped through all your hoops, and agreed to your job offer. She's ready to start caring for your child. Wait! Is she really ready?

When *you* start a position with a new company, chances are you have a period of orientation and training. Your employer may provide you with a checklist of procedures you are to follow and areas of responsibility that are clearly yours. In order to ensure your success, the company provides everything it can to get you started in the right direction.

Smart companies know that good training programs lead to productive, happy employees. Ultimately that results in less turnover and lower hiring costs. The same formula applies to your new nanny.

Most parents spend a day or two at home with a new nanny explaining where things are and what is expected. Use this time to train your nanny, using the same professionalism you expect from her. This is the logical end to your extensive screening and hiring process. Rather than playing it by ear and hoping that you are able to cover everything, use this chapter to structure the training time.

Child Care: Safety and Duties

Review the specific duties and safety procedures you expect your nanny to perform as they relate to the care of your child. Do not assume anything! For example, in years past, mothers and caregivers were told to put babies to sleep on the stomach, to avoid choking and possible sudden infant death syndrome (SIDS). In 1997, the "Back to Sleep" campaign instructed parents and caregivers to put a baby to sleep on the back. The new campaign has reduced SIDS deaths by almost 40 percent.

Things change. Don't assume that a grandmotherly nanny with her years of experience, or even a younger nanny just out of school, is current on today's child care guidelines.

Safety: Discuss Basic Safety Guidelines

- ◼ Review CPR techniques.

- ◼ Review the Heimlich maneuver.

- ◼ Review pool safety rules. *Never, ever* leave a child unattended in the yard or near water of any kind.

- ◼ Review kitchen safety rules.

- ◼ Review bathing rules. *Never, ever* leave a child unattended in the bath.

- ◼ Give your nanny a list of emergency numbers on a 3 x 5 card for her purse. Put another copy in the diaper bag. Post a third copy near the telephone.

Meal Preparation: Discuss Preferences and Planning

- ◼ Explain your child's likes and dislikes.

- ◼ Outline mealtime choices you prefer.

- ◼ Discuss healthy snacks.

- ◼ Concerning grocery shopping, explain your procedure for maintaining item lists, budgeting, and paying for groceries.

- ◼ Discuss with your nanny which meals you will provide for her. (Most parents provide live-out nannies with lunch.)

Planning Activities: Discuss What Activities You Expect

■ Reading should be a part of every day your nanny spends with your child. Suggest a weekly trip to the library for the children's story hour and book selection. Provide her with the library's schedule or phone number.

■ Suggest various craft ideas that are age-appropriate for your child. You might even purchase a workbook of ideas at a teacher's supply store to encourage your nanny in this area. Prepare a box of craft supplies and ask her to suggest any other items she may need.

■ Help your nanny to set up play dates with other children and nannies in your neighborhood. A weekly "date" lasting an hour or two is good for both nannies and children.

■ Exercise is important! Suggest that your nanny plan a 15- to 20-minute period each day that includes physical activity. This may be a brisk walk, climbing the monkey bars at the park, dancing to music at home, or just running around in the backyard.

■ Encourage your nanny also to schedule quiet time every day. The children can play quietly while the nanny takes a break—always with the children in her sight.

Provide your nanny with a weekly planner or organizer to help her schedule all the suggestions above.

Other Duties: Discuss Any Additional Duties

■ Children's rooms. Show the nanny where the things are located in the children's bedrooms and what areas she is to maintain. Usually, the nanny keeps the room tidy, changes the bedclothes, and keeps supplies in stock.

■ Family areas. If the nanny is to care for other areas of the home or if she is required to do family laundry, explain *specifically* what is expected and how you would like to see the task completed. The more specific you are now, the less chance for confusion and problems later.

■ Help your nanny do a better job with your children by helping her to understand them better. Discuss:

> Favorite toys
> Favorite songs
> Fears
> Motivation
> Anticipated problems
> Strengths
> Weaknesses
> Nap routine
> Meal routine

■ Discipline is an issue that must be clearly addressed. Explain to your nanny what steps she should take when your child misbehaves. Make sure that she is consistent with *your* methods. Reinforce the point that at no time is she to strike your child or demean your child verbally. Positive discipline is best.

Nanny Performance Reviews

As an employer, you should take time to comment on your employee's performance, pointing out what she is doing right as well as areas for improvement. Eventually, this will also be an appropriate time to recognize good work with an increase in pay or a bonus.

After your nanny's first week of work, chances are that both of you will want to clarify certain aspects of the job. She may want you to review just how you want her to handle your 2-year-old's tantrums. You may want to remind her about your child's nap routine. Make time to sit down, without the children underfoot, to discuss or clarify these issues.

If you have an area of concern and aren't sure how to approach it, start with a positive comment first so that the nanny doesn't feel she is being criticized. You might begin with, "I really like the fact that you're taking the children to the park each day. By the way, please make sure they have on their jackets each time they go out."

Sit down again after the first month to review her performance with her and ask if she would like to discuss anything of concern.

Use the *Nanny Performance Review* form (page 70) to help you through this process.

Nanny Performance Review

Nanny's name:

Date of hire:

Parent's name:

Date of review:

Performance Area	Excellent	Fair	Needs Improvement
Punctuality Arrives for work on time, ready to take over the care of the children.	——	——	——
Child care Consistently provides quality care and supervision for the children.	——	——	——
Additional duties Completes additional assigned duties (housework, etc.) on time and according to instructions.	——	——	——
Role modeling Provides a strong and positive adult role model for the children.	——	——	——
Nurturing Provides positive reinforcement and helps build self-esteem in the children.	——	——	——
Creativity Plans educational and fun activities on a regular basis.	——	——	——
Discipline Handles discipline according to methods previously agreed upon.	——	——	——
Reading Reads to or listens to children read on a regular basis.	——	——	——

Areas of concern:_____

Review the ground rules with your nanny and allow her to comment on any of the issues below:

Privacy
Are you each respecting the other's privacy? Do you need to establish more specific schedules with regard to how much time you spend with each other versus private family time? (For the live-in nanny.)

Telephone
Is the phone being used according to guidelines previously agreed on? Are there too many long-distance calls? Does the nanny spend too much time on the phone?

Television
Is the television or the stereo being used according to previously established guidelines? (Type of programming or music, volume, and amount of usage.)

Meal planning
Are nutritionally sound meals and snacks for the kids the norm? Do you need to clarify your preferences? Have you clearly established your nanny's "allowances" in the kitchen?

New goals
Establish any new goals and objectives for your nanny here:

_____

_____

Nanny's comments

_____

_____

Was an increase in salary awarded at this time?　　❑　Yes　　❑　No

If yes, how much?　$_____ increase per week, effective _____.

New salary is now　$_____ per week.

Next scheduled review date: _____

_____　　_____
Parent's signature　　　　　　　　　　　　Date

_____　　_____
Nanny's signature　　　　　　　　　　　　Date

Video Surveillance

Several years ago, a network magazine program reported on parents who used tiny cameras to secretly videotape their nannies interacting with their children. The results were dramatic. Footage of nannies abusing children, cursing at them, and also neglecting them began to appear on every newscast and talk show. As a result, an entire industry was born—at-home spy technology.

Opinions vary on the question of whether secret surveillance is ethical. Some people feel strongly that it is an invasion of the nanny's privacy. Others feel that if you don't trust a nanny, you should fire her rather than bait her with your child.

On the other hand, there is simply no way of knowing what really happens when you walk out of that front door. Obviously an infant can't articulate what happens during the course of the day. Even a toddler, who can begin to express concerns, is still too young to discern what is appropriate or inappropriate behavior on the part of a caregiver. After days or months, the child may begin to assume that even though mommy doesn't curse at me, it must be okay for the nanny to do so.

Certainly coming home unannounced for a "spot check" is a good idea, but a nanny's behavior may change when you walk in. The only way a parent really knows what is going on while he or she is away is by videotaping.

Parents who have used video surveillance have had amazing results. According to a national nanny surveillance company, between 60 and 70 percent of parents who videotape their nannies end up firing the nanny—some for abuse, most for neglect.

One mother found that as soon as she left, the nanny put the baby in the high chair next to the kitchen table where she began preparing lines of cocaine to snort. Another mother's camera caught her nanny stealing food from the pantry each day and putting it into the trunk of her car. Yet another found that while her child received excellent care from the nanny, the nanny could be heard telling the toddler, "I take much better care of you than your mother."

Nannies have been found talking on the phone while a baby crawled out of the room, out of sight! Others have been caught sleeping while children toddled around the house unattended.

On the other hand, some parents have put their mind at ease, knowing that their children are being well cared for. One new mom found that the nanny went to great lengths to stop her 6-week-old baby from crying upon waking from her nap. The nanny sang to the baby, rocked her, danced with her. Mom knew from experience that all her baby wanted was the bottle. She was able to tell the nanny the next day that it was a good idea to have the bottle ready so that when the baby woke up, she would have what she really wanted. This mother was delighted with the results of her taping.

However, the legality of secret surveillance could be an issue. The federal wiretapping law prohibits taping the conversation of another person without that person's consent. This law was in effect prior to the advent of video technology, so it addressed only audiotaping. As of now, the legality of secret video surveillance has not been tested in the courts.

It's advisable to contact your local district attorney for advice, as local laws may supersede federal laws in this area. Many local authorities have stated that videotaping (without the audio portion) is legal if done in the area that is considered the work area—the baby's room, the family room, or the kitchen—and if the taping is done for security reasons. A camera in the nanny's room or the nanny's bath is probably a violation of privacy.

It's a good idea to either draft a release or add to the work agreement a statement by the nanny that she gives you permission to tape her on the job without her knowledge of the time or day of taping.

Firing a Nanny

She just isn't working out. You have a knot in your stomach each morning as you kiss your child good-bye and hand him or her over to your nanny. It no longer feels right. It's time to fire the nanny.

You thought hiring was complicated! Your strategy for letting a nanny go can be just as difficult. You want to minimize your time away from work to handle this crisis. You hope to ease your child's transition from nanny to nanny. How do you interview new nannies without your current nanny finding out?

What do you do if *she* gets upset? This can be a real concern, especially if your nanny lives with you. Not only will she no longer have a job, but you are taking away her home. This can make a bad situation worse.

One mother of three, with lots of experience with nannies, learned the hard way. "I no longer give my nannies notice of their termination," she said. "I gave one nanny two weeks' notice only to have her steal clothes, jewelry, and cash!" This mother tried to collect for damages but was unable to do so. "I had to take two weeks off from work to handle the theft, to regroup, and to train a new nanny."

Tips for Firing a Nanny

■ **Do not give the nanny "notice" of her termination.**
Have a paycheck ready for all wages due at the time you let her go.

■ **You may or may not want to give her the reason for termination.**
If the reason for her termination is one that may agitate her or put your child, home, or fam-

ily at risk, it may be enough to say simply, "We've had a change in child care plans." You could add that your aunt has agreed to watch the baby, for instance.

- **Ask the nanny to sign a statement indicating her last day worked and noting that payment was received.**
  Ask her to sign the statement, and then you'll hand her the paycheck. This will protect you from a claim for nonpayment of wages, a situation that carries stiff penalties.

- **Change the locks on your doors and the codes to your alarm systems.**
  Even if the nanny lives out, chances are you have given her a key to your home. She may have made a copy of that key, in case she lost yours.

- **Change school emergency cards.**
  Take the nanny off the list of individuals who are allowed to pick up your child from school. Notify the office staff and the teachers of preschools and elementary schools that the nanny is no longer authorized to have contact with your children. If you suspect that there might be a problem, request that your child meet the new nanny in the school office for the after-school pickup.

- **Change telephone calling card numbers.**
  Did your nanny have access to your calling card PIN code for emergency phone calls? You will want to make sure you change the PIN code for your telephone account as well as any other accounts she had access to.

- **Circulate her photograph.**
  It's to be hoped that you took a photograph of your nanny during her first few days. If not, you should have a copy of her photo ID from the preemployment process. Let the neighbors see the photo and alert them that she has no reason to be at or near your home or with or near your children. If they see her, instruct them to contact the police. Also, show the photo to the new nanny so that she can recognize the former nanny, who may come to your home or approach your children at the park.

- **Talk to your children.**
  Tell your children that they now have a new nanny. The former nanny is no longer the person they are to listen to. Instruct them never to go anywhere with the former nanny unless you have told them it is okay.

■ **Talk to the new nanny.**

Explain to the new nanny what went wrong with the old nanny. You don't want to repeat the same mistakes. If your child bonded with the former nanny, the transition between nannies may take some time. Spending time with your child and the new nanny together will ease the transition.

Child-Abuse Awareness

It's every parent's worst nightmare—signs of abuse at the hands of the child's caregiver. According to the U.S. Advisory Board on Child Abuse, in the United States, five children die *each day* at the hands of their parents or caregivers. More preschool children die from abuse or neglect than from falls, choking, drowning, or fires.

Child Help USA reports that abuse is usually caused by a person close to the child—a parent, a relative, or a caregiver—and seldom by a stranger.

You can approach this subject with your nanny in a nonthreatening way by sitting down to discuss the signs of abuse with her. Explain that since she is caring for your child for most of the day, she should immediately report it to you if she sees the following signs of abuse. These signs can suggest abuse at the hands of anyone—such as a preschool teacher or even the child's friends. In this way, the nanny is aware that *you* are aware of these signs. This may deter any potential abuse.

Signs of Physical Abuse

- Bruises or welts that appear to be caused by an object (a stick, a buckle, a belt, a hairbrush).

- Bruises on the body in places that would not normally be affected by the everyday falls a child may have. For example, it would be normal to see bruises on the child's knees and elbows, and perhaps even on the forehead. But bruises around the eyes, mouth, back, buttocks, genitals, thighs, or calves would be suspicious. These areas are not normally bruised when a child falls.

Signs of Neglect

- A hungry child.

- A dirty child.

- Clothing unsuitable for the weather or the activity.

- Abnormal or antisocial behavior; withdrawal or depression.

Signs of Sexual Abuse

- Child expresses interest in inappropriate activity with an adult.

- Clothing that is torn or bloody.

- Reports of pain, bleeding, itching, or bruising in the genital area.

Conclusion

The Nanny Kit has provided you with the information and tools you need to find, hire, and happily retain your own nanny. The goal of this book is to empower parents to provide the right care for their children.

The author would appreciate your comments and experiences with putting the information in *The Nanny Kit* to use. Please contact her at this address:

Kimberly A. Porrazzo
Southern California Nanny Center
P.O. Box 663
Lake Forest, CA 92630
E-mail: porrazzo@ix.netcom.com
www.sandcastleweb.com/nanny

A note on Child Help USA: Please consider assisting those children less fortunate than your own who are victims of child abuse, by donating to this worthy organization. By purchasing this workbook, you have already made a contribution, as a portion of the profits are dedicated to Child Help. Contact Child Help at (800) 422-4453.

Resources

Parents who hire a nanny on their own may turn to advisers and services to assist them. Some of the resources listed below are also utilized by nanny agencies. These resources include industry associations, companies that specialize in conducting background investigations, nanny payroll and tax services, and video surveillance companies.

Here are several resources to consider.

✎ **Southern California Nanny Center**
P.O. Box 663
Lake Forest, CA 92630
www.sandcastleweb.com/nanny
Provides information and resources for parents all over the country who hire and employ nannies. Acts as a "parent advocate," assisting parents with the proper way to hire and manage in-home child care. News and information on website are free.

✎ **International Nanny Association**
900 Haddon Avenue, Suite 438
Collingswood, NJ 08108
(609) 858-0808
fax: (609) 858-2519
www.nanny.org
A membership organization that supports nanny agencies, nannies, nanny educators, and others serving the nanny industry. Provides parents with tips for hiring and employing nannies.

A Naninet

www.nannynetwork.com

Provides a free online database of companies across the country that assist parents seeking in-home child care. Companies are not endorsed by the organization.

 Nanitax

2 Pidgeon Hill Drive, Suite 210

Sterling, VA 20165

(800) NANITAX

www.4nannytaxes.com

Assists parents with a fee-based program that handles the preparation and filing of the required tax forms for domestic employees. Website features a Nanitax Calculator, an online newsletter, and nanny tax tips.

 GTM Associates

16 Computer Drive West

Albany, NY 12205

888 4-EASYPAY

www.gtmassoc.com

For a fee, provides nanny payroll and tax services for parents with domestic employees.

 California Trustline Registry

744 P Street, M.S. 19-57

Sacramento, CA 95814

(800) 822-8490 (inside California)

(415) 882-0234 (outside California)

www.trustline.org

For a fee, conducts background checks on nannies in California, including a criminal check, child-abuse index check, DMV report, and more. Parents can request a background check or verify a nanny's claim that she is already a "Trustline provider." Also provides national FBI check for additional charge. All California nanny agencies must clear nannies they place through Trustline.

Child Care Registry
3494 Camino Tassajara Road, Suite 243
Danville, CA 94506
(510) 248-4100

For a fee, provides parents anywhere in the United States with a national background check on nanny candidates within 48 hours.

 Eisenberg Associates
1340 Centre Street, Suite 203
Newton Centre, MA 02159
(800) 777-5765

Provides health insurance, disability insurance, and financial programs for nannies.

 Immigration and Naturalization Service (INS)
(800) 755-0777

Provides an employer's handbook concerning how to verify a nanny's legal right to work in the United States. Also provides the INS I-9 form.

 Internal Revenue Service (IRS)—Forms
(800) TAX-FORM

Provides parents with information on tax requirements for domestic employees. Form No. 926, Household Employer's Tax Guide, details what is required.

 Internal Revenue Service (IRS)—Questions
(800) TAX-1040

Provides answers to questions on tax requirements for domestic employers.

 Babywatch Corporation
(800) 558-5669

Provides video surveillance equipment for parents wishing to secretly tape a nanny on the job. This corporation has representatives all over the country.

Index

NOTE: Italicized page numbers refer to forms.